Presented to:

_____

A Gift From:

_____

Date:

_____

Also by Jim Coy...

The ABCs of Matthew for Kids
ISBN 978158169-3188

Matthew A to Z + 2 (for adults)
ISBN 978158169-2761

Valor (A Gathering of Eagles Series)
ISBN 158169-1114

Prisoners of Hope (A Gathering of Eagles Series)
ISBN 158169-1777

A Gathering of Eagles II
ISBN 158169-0495

THE MIRACLES OF JESUS

for kids

Jim and Vicki Coy

The Miracles of Jesus for Kids
by Jim and Vicki Coy
Copyright ©2010 Jim and Vicki Coy

ISBN 978-1-58169-3515
For Worldwide Distribution
Printed in the U.S.A.

Artwork by Masaru Horie

Evergreen Press
P.O. Box 191540 • Mobile, AL 36619
800-367-8203

Dedication

This book is dedicated to every parent, grandparent, and teacher who would like to teach their children, grandchildren, and students about the miracles of Jesus Christ.

Introduction

There are at least thirty-six miracles in the Gospels that Bible scholars agree happened during the earthly ministry of Christ.

The greatest miracle is not turning water into wine; it is not walking on water, stilling the storm, or even raising the dead. The greatest miracle is the miracle of a changed heart!

NATURAL MIRACLES

Jesus Calms the Storm

One day, Jesus was out in a boat with His disciples when a really bad storm blew in. The disciples became frightened and called out to Jesus. He woke up and rebuked the winds and the sea, and there was a great calm. Even the winds obeyed Jesus! *Matthew 8:26*

(See Matthew 8:23-27, Mark 4:35-41, and Luke 8:22-25.)

Jesus Feeds 5000

A very large crowd of people had followed Jesus to hear Him teach. It was getting late in the day so His disciples said, "Send them into the villages to get some food." Jesus said, "Don't send them away. Give them food to eat." Then Jesus took five loaves and two fish, multiplied them, and fed them all! *Matthew 14:16*

(See Matthew 14:15-21, Mark 6:34-44, Luke 9:12-17, John 6:5-12.)

Jesus Walks on Water...Peter Too!

Another day the disciples were out on a lake. It got really stormy and the disciples were frightened. Walking on the water, Jesus went to them. Peter said, "Is that You, Lord?" Jesus said, "Come." So Peter jumped out of the boat and walked on the water too. *Matthew 14:25*

(See Matthew 14:24-27, Mark 6:45-51, John 6:16-24.)

Jesus Feeds 4000

Another time the people followed Jesus for three days and were very hungry because they had nothing to eat. Jesus had compassion on them and didn't want to send them away hungry. He took seven loaves and a few small fish, gave thanks, gave some to His disciples who fed the others, and they all ate. The leftovers filled seven baskets! *Matthew 15:36–37*

(See Matthew 15:32-38, Mark 8:4-9.)

He Got a Coin From a Fish!

Jesus told Peter that His disciples should pay their taxes. Then He said, "Go fishing! Take the first fish you catch, open its mouth, and you will find a coin to pay our taxes." *Matthew 17:27*

(See Matthew 17:24-27.)

Jesus Curses the Fig Tree

Jesus was headed back to the city when He became hungry. He saw a fig tree and hoped to get a snack, but the fig tree had no figs. Jesus said, "Let no more food grow on this fig tree." The tree withered so quickly that His disciples were amazed. *Matthew 21:19*

(See Matthew 21:17-20, Mark 11:12-14.)

A Miraculous Catch of Fish

Many of Jesus' followers were fishermen. One day, He told Peter to "Take the boat out into the deeper water and let down your nets." Peter caught so many fish the net was about to break! Jesus said, "Don't be afraid. From now on you will fish for men." *Luke 5:4*

(See Luke 5:2-9.)

Jesus Turns Water Into Wine

Jesus, His disciples, and His mother were invited to attend a wedding feast in Cana. But the wine ran out and Jesus' mother, Mary, asked Him to help them. Jesus said, "Fill the pots with water, then pour the water out and take it to the master of the feast." When the master of the feast tasted the water that had been turned into wine, he was amazed at how good it tasted. *John 2:7-8*

(See John 2:3-8.)

Another Miraculous Catch

After a long night of fishing, Jesus' disciples had caught nothing. Jesus said, "Cast your net on the right side of the boat. You will catch fish." They caught so many fish they couldn't bring the net into their boat. *John 21:6*

(See John 21:3-6.)

HEALING MIRACLES

Jesus Cleanses a Leper

A leper came to Jesus and bowed before Him saying, "If You are willing, heal me." Jesus touched the leper, saying, "I am willing. Be clean!" And the man was immediately healed. *Matthew 8:3*

(See Matthew 8:2-4, Mark 1:40-45, Luke 5:12-14.)

Jesus Heals the Centurion's Servant

A centurion came to Jesus and asked Him to heal his servant. Jesus said, "I will go and heal him." But the centurion said, "You don't have to go, just say the word and he will be healed." Jesus said, "Go! As you have believed, it will be done." The centurion's servant was healed, and Jesus was amazed at the man's faith. *Matthew 8:13*

(See Matthew 8:5-13, Luke 7:2-10.)

19

Jesus Heals Peter's Mother~in~Law

When Jesus came to Peter's house, He saw that Peter's mother-in-law was very sick. So He touched her hand, and the fever left her. *Matthew 8:15*

(See Matthew 8:14-15, Mark 1:29-31, Luke 4:38-39.)

Jesus Heals the Sick and Oppressed

After Jesus healed Peter's mother-in-law, the people brought Him many who were sick. He cast out the evil spirits with a word, and He healed all who were sick. This fulfilled the Scriptures about Jesus. *Matthew 8:16*

(See Matthew 8:, Mark 1:32-34, Luke 4:40-41.)

Jesus Heals a Paralytic

One day Jesus was teaching in someone's home. The friends of a paralyzed man couldn't get in to bring him to Jesus so they let him down through a hole in the roof. Jesus said to the paralyzed man, "Arise, take up your bed, and go to your home." *Matthew 9:6*

(See Matthew 9:2-7, Mark 2:2-12, Luke 5:18-24.)

Jesus Heals the Bleeding Woman

While Jesus was going down the road, a woman came up behind Him. She had a serious bleeding problem for twelve years, but the doctors couldn't help her. She said to herself, "If I just touch the edge of His robe, I will be healed." When she touched His robe, Jesus felt power go out from Him. He turned to her and said, "Daughter, your faith has made you whole." *Matthew 9:22*

(See Matthew 9:20-22, Mark 5:24-34, Luke 8:43-48.)

Jesus Heals Two Blind Men

Two blind men were following Jesus and saying, "Have mercy on us." He asked if they believed that He could heal them, and they said, "Yes!" Jesus touched their eyes, and at once their eyes were opened, and they could see. *Matthew 9:29-30*

(See Matthew 9:27-31.)

Jesus Heals a Withered Hand

Jesus went to the synagogue one Sabbath day and found a man there with a withered hand. The Pharisees wanted to trap Jesus so they asked Him if it was lawful to heal on the Sabbath. But Jesus asked if they would rescue one of their sheep that had fallen into a pit on the Sabbath. When they said nothing, Jesus said, "Stretch out your hand," and the man's hand was restored and made whole. *Matthew 12:13*

(See Matthew 12:10-13, Mark 3:1-5, Luke 6:16-10.)

The Woman With Great Faith

A woman came to Jesus to beg Him to heal her daughter. When He saw her faith He said, "O woman, great is your faith: it will be as you have asked." And her daughter was healed that very hour. *Matthew 15:28*

(See Matthew 15:22-28, Mark 7:24-30.)

Jesus Heals an Epileptic Boy

A man came to Jesus and knelt before Him. He said, "Have mercy on my son and heal him. He is an epileptic, and he often falls into the fire or water. I brought him to Your disciples, but they could not heal him." Jesus rebuked the demon, and it left; and the child was instantly cured. Then Jesus said, "If you have faith as small as a mustard seed, you will be able to move mountains!" *Matthew 17:18*

(See Matthew 17:14-18, Mark 9:17-29, Luke 9:38-42.)

Jesus Heals Blind Bartimaeus

One day Jesus was going down the road. When a blind man heard it was Jesus, he cried out, "Have mercy on me!" Some told him to be quiet, but Jesus asked him to come to Him, and He healed his sight. *Mark 10:46*

(See Mark 10:46-52, Luke 18:35-43.)

Jesus Heals a Deaf Mute

The people brought a man who could not speak or hear to Jesus to be healed. Jesus took the man aside and put His fingers in his ears. Then He spit and touched his tongue. Jesus said, "Be opened!" The man's ears were opened, his tongue was loosed, and he was able to hear clearly and speak plainly. *Mark 7:35*

(See Mark 7:32-37.)

Jesus Heals a Blind Man

When Jesus came to a town called Bethsaida, the people brought a blind man to Him. Jesus put spit on his eyes, and he could see shadows. Then He put his hands on the man's eyes again, and he could see clearly. *Mark 8:23-25*

(See Mark 8:22-26.)

Jesus Heals a Deformity

Jesus was teaching in one of the synagogues on a Sabbath day. He saw a woman who had been bent over for 18 years—she could not stand straight at all. Jesus called her forward and said to her, "Woman, you are healed of your sickness." Then He put His hands on her, and immediately she straightened up and praised God. *Luke 13:12*

(See Luke 13:11-13.)

Jesus Heals a Man With Dropsy

Jesus went to the house of a Pharisee, and they brought a man to Him who had severe swelling. Jesus asked the Pharisees if it was lawful to heal on the Sabbath. They were silent. Jesus healed him and let him go. *Luke 14:2-4*

(See Luke 14:2-4.)

Jesus Heals Ten Lepers

When Jesus was on His way to Jerusalem, ten lepers called out to Him from a distance in a loud voice, "Jesus have mercy on us!" When Jesus saw them He said, "Go show yourselves to the priests"; and as they went, they were cleansed from their leprosy. But only one came back to thank Jesus. He asked, "Where are the other nine?" *Luke 17:12-14*

(See Luke 17:12-19.)

Jesus Heals the Servant's Ear

The night a crowd came to arrest Jesus, one of His disciples struck the servant of the high priest and cut off his ear. Jesus touched his ear and healed him. Jesus even healed those who were about to crucify Him! *Luke 22:50-51*

(See Luke 22:45-51.)

Jesus Heals the Official's Son

When Jesus went to Cana in Galilee, a government official came to Him. The official's son was near death, and he begged Jesus to go down to Capernaum and heal his son. Jesus said, "Unless you people see signs and wonders, you will never believe." But the official insisted that Jesus go. Jesus said, "Go, your son will live." The official took Jesus at His word, and his son was healed. *John 4:50*

(See John 4:47-53.)

Jesus Heals a Crippled Man

A man crippled for 38 years waited by the pool of Bethesda for the water to be stirred. When Jesus saw him He asked, "Do you want to be healed?" Jesus said, "Rise, take up your bed and walk." *John 5:8*

(See John 5:5-9.)

Jesus Heals a Man Born Blind

As Jesus walked along, He saw a man who was blind from birth. His disciples asked Jesus if he was blind because his parents had sinned against God. Jesus said, "Neither this man nor his parents sinned. He was born blind so that God's work would be shown in his life." So Jesus made some mud with His spit and put it on the man's eyes. Then He said, "Go wash in the pool of Siloam." The blind man went and washed and came back seeing. *John 9:7*

(See John 9:1-25.)

RAISING THE DEAD

Jesus Brings a Girl Back to Life

One day a ruler came to Jesus and asked Him to lay His hand on his daughter because she had just died. When Jesus entered the ruler's house, the mourners were very loud. Jesus said, "Go away; the young girl is not dead but is asleep." After the people left, Jesus took her by the hand, and the child arose. News of the miracle spread through the whole region. *Matthew 9:25*

(See Matthew 9:18-19, 23-25, Mark 5:21-25, 35-43, Luke 8:41-43, 49-50.)

Jesus Raises a Widow's Son

When Jesus and His disciples were visiting the town of Nain, there was a funeral procession. The mother of the dead man was crying. He had been her only son, and she was a widow. When Jesus saw her, His heart went out to her. He said, "Don't cry." Then he touched the coffin and said, "Young man, I say to you, arise." The dead man sat up and started talking to his mother. *Luke 7:14*

(See Luke 7:11-15.)

Jesus Raises Lazarus From the Dead

Jesus loved his friends Mary, Martha, and Lazarus. When Lazarus got very sick, Mary and Martha asked Jesus to come to Bethany to heal him. But Jesus waited until Lazarus had died so that He could do an even greater miracle. When Jesus got to the tomb, He said, "Lazarus, come out." Then Lazarus came back to life and came out! *John 11:43*

(See John 11:1-44.)

CASTING OUT
DEMONS

Jesus Casts the Demons Into Pigs

After the storm, when Jesus and His disciples came to the other side of the lake, two demon-possessed men came out from the tombs to meet Him. The demons shouted at Jesus, "Have you come here to torment us? If you cast us out, send us into the herd of pigs." He said to the demons, "Go," and they went into the herd of pigs, which ran into the lake and drowned. *Matthew 8:32*

(See Matthew 8:28-32, Mark 5:1-13, Luke 8:26-33.)

Jesus Casts Out a Deaf Spirit

Jesus was leaving a town when they brought a demon-possessed man who could not speak. When the demon was cast out, the man was able to speak, and the crowd was amazed! *Matthew 9:33*

(See Matthew 9:32-33.)

Jesus Rebukes an Evil Spirit

Jesus and His disciples went to Capernaum and entered the synagogue where He began to teach. The people were amazed because Jesus taught with authority. Just then, a man who was possessed by an evil spirit cried out, "Have You come to destroy us? I know You are God's Holy One!" Jesus rebuked the evil spirit saying, "Be quiet! Come out of him!" And the spirit came out. *Mark 1:23-25*

(See Mark 1:23-26, Luke 4:33-35.)

Jesus Casts Out a Demon

The people brought a demon-possessed man, who was blind and unable to speak, to Jesus. Jesus healed him so that he could both see and speak. The people were astonished! *Matthew 12:22*

(See Matthew 12:22, Luke 11:14.)

Index & Summary

About the Authors

Jim Coy and his wife, Vicki, have three children: Tim, Patricia, and Josh. Jim and Vicki attend New Life Community Church in Columbia, Missouri. They are Associate staff with the Military Ministry of Campus Crusade for Christ.

To contact the authors:
www.agatheringofeagles.com
coyjv@socket.net

Artwork by Masaru Horie
www.christiancliparts.net